I Know a Scientist

Jean Feldman and Holly Karapetkova

Tune: I Had a Little Turtle

www.rourkeclassroom.com

I know a scientist
And you can be one, too!
Here's the **scientific method.**
So you'll know what to do.

First you find a **question.**

Just take a look around.

What is it that you want to know?

Now you write it down.

Next you make a guess.

It's called a hypothesis.

About what will happen,

When you do your tests.

Now **experiment.**

Observe it, write it, too.

You'll need lots of data,

To show your guess is true.

Draw your **conclusions.**

Look into any doubts.

Then tell everybody,

What you've found out!

$E=mc^2$

Scientific Method

1 **Question**

What do you want to know?

2 **Hypothesis**

What do you think will happen?

3 **Experiment**

Test to see if your guess is right!

4 **Conclusion**

Tell what you found out!